Right Brain
Brain
Red

HAPPY DAY'
CHRISTIAN

Right *Pay*

Brain

Red

7 Ideas
for Creative
Success

Reyn Guyer

with Tim Walsh

RIVER GROVE
BOOKS

Published by River Grove Books
Austin, TX
www.rivergrovebooks.com

Distributed by River Grove Books

Design and composition by Greenleaf Book Group, Sheila Parr, and Curt Cruz
Cover design by Greenleaf Book Group and Sheila Parr
AUTH Cartoon, Uncle Sam playing Middle East Twister from The Philadelphia Inquirer July 23, 2003. Copyright © 2003 by The Philadelphia Inquirer. All rights reserved. Reprinted by permission of Universal Uclick.
Cartoon, "Well!" from For Better or For Worse by Lynn Johnston. Copyright © 1989 by Lynn Johnston Productions. Distributed by Universal Uclick. All rights reserved. Reprinted by permission of Universal Uclick.
Cartoon, "The department budget cut back on breathalyzers," by Gary McCoy. Copyright © by Gary McCoy. Reprinted by permission.

Cataloging-in-Publication data is available.

Print ISBN: 978-1-63299-073-0

eBook ISBN: 978-1-63299-074-7

First Edition

This book and most all the opportunities that have graced my life would not have come to be without my steady, constant, and very perceptive life partner, Mary. Her beauty shines from deep within her and is a real source of inspiration every day.

Many thanks to Daly Walker, whose encouragement and counsel spawned this book. And thanks to Tim Walsh, my patient friend.

CREATE + DO = SUCCESS

Contents

I have been a part of many teams over the years, and in this chapter I share what the successful ones have had in common.

Open your meetings and your mind with these three magic words. They have worked wonders for me.

Some of the biggest breakthroughs in business have come about because a maverick took a long look at a company, industry, or even societal rule and wondered, "What happens if we break it?"

Breakthrough ideas often come from where we least expect them. An outsider to any industry thinks differently from those on the inside, and that outsider perspective often creates something exciting.

Idea #5: Make It Real: Make One!

My response to aspiring inventors who want to tell me about their great product idea is "Don't tell me. Make one!"

Idea #6: Be Open
If we stay curious and open to opportunity, new doors open to us.

Idea #7: Finding The Rush
The excitement that a fresh new idea brings is what keeps me coming back to my drawing board.

About the Authors

Preface

I first met Reyn Guyer in 2003 when I was research-
ing my book *Timeless Toys*. At the time, I knew Reyn
only as the inventor of the game Twister and the
NERF line of toys. I soon found out that Reyn dis-
liked being referred to as "the inventor" and was
quick to point out instead that he was the leader of
the teams that created those iconic playthings. Since
then, the more time I've spent with Reyn, the more
I've become aware that he is a very humble man—
much happier to talk about the accomplishments of
others than to tout his own successes. Whenever we
connected over the next six years, through an occa-
sional phone call or chance run-in at a trade show,
the context was always toys. It wasn't until I set foot
in his design studio that I discovered there is much
more to Reyn Guyer than Twister and NERF.

In 2009, I arranged to bring a film crew to
Reyn's home to interview him for the documentary film *Toyland*. As I ascended the stairs to his loft
studio, familiar faces caught my eye. Carrie Underwood smiled on the cover of her multiplatinum
record *Carnival Ride*. Kenny Chesney peered out

from under his black cowboy hat on the cover of the triple-platinum record *No Shoes, No Shirt, No Problems.* I caught glimpses of Reba McEntire, Allison Krause, and more, all on the covers of shiny silver records.

"Reyn, what's with all the record awards?" I asked incredulously.

His response was typical understated Reyn: "Oh, my daughter Ree and I formed a music publishing company, and we've had some success."

Some success?! Frame after frame of platinum and multiplatinum awards lined the walls.

Reyn's studio was filled with original oil paintings, framed poems, toy prototypes, and other evidence of creativity set in motion. And another surprise: On a high shelf sat a slick-looking package with a logo that read The Sonday System.

I asked Reyn about it, and he replied, "We developed a tutoring system that any reader can use to help students who are struggling to read get caught up to their peers. We're in 1,800 school systems around the country."

The seeds of the book you're holding took root that day.

Imagine learning product design from the originator of brands that have generated over $8 billion in sales. Could you gain business insights from someone whose company stormed the cutthroat music industry as an outsider and who now has a

Grammy award, two CMA Song of the Year awards, and forty-six charted singles on the country and pop music charts? How would you like to pick the brain of a rule breaker who overcame dyslexia and formed a learning company that has given the gift of literacy to 500,000 students all over the world? Now what if all three of those people were the same man?

In addition to immensely popular toys and games, Reyn has created the Wrensong/Reynsong Music publishing company, the Winsor Learning company, the musical drama *Stained Glass*, the New-Age/jazz album *Lyrias*, the children's stories and songs of Curly Lasagna, dozens of paintings and sculptures held in private collections across the country, and more!

Reyn Guyer has been wildly successful in multiple creative fields. In this book, he shares some of the ideas that have helped him get there. I consider convincing Reyn to write this book a great success of my own. If you're on a quest to create, you couldn't learn from a better teacher.

Tim Walsh
October 2015
Sarasota, Florida

Introduction

I am a very lucky man. I've been blessed with good health; my amazing life partner of fifty-eight years, Mary; five children; ten grandchildren; and two great-grandchildren.

But my good fortune doesn't stop there. For reasons that I'm still trying to figure out, I have been blessed with the ability to bring many new ideas into the world. I truly believe that every one of us who lives and breathes is creative. Each of us is working out life's problems and opportunities—or the lack thereof—in our own unique way. In this book, we will explore together how doing—taking action, making a working model—is attached to being creative by an umbilical cord. *Right Brain Red* is about what has worked for me and how I've managed to turn my creative rush into business and artistic success: "The Rush" is what I believe each of us feels when we're in the process of creating something. It's the inherent joy and inspiration we get from working on what we love.

In 1965, I was working in the design firm that I co-owned with my father. We created point-of-purchase displays for various large companies, but I wasn't convinced we had a good business model. And certainly on a daily basis, I didn't feel The Rush. So I started branching out. My first big success was a game that started as a promotional product for shoe polish but that ultimately became the classic party game Twister.

I eventually split off from Reynolds Guyer Agency of Design (named after my father) to form Winsor Concepts, where I could focus on game and toy development. Winsor Concepts was the second team I built around what I now see clearly as my search for The Rush. Eventually, my search led our team to bounce packing foam around the office. We quickly realized how fun it was to break the ubiquitous household rule of "no playing ball in the house"—and NERF was born.

Music has always been another creative outlet for me. When I was just six years old, my mother, father, and I would harmonize around the family piano. As long as I can remember, I've been writing and performing original songs. In the early 1980s I was recording some of my songs with local musicians, and my daughter Ree decided that they were good enough to sell. Soon enough, we were in the music business. Wrensong, the Nashville-based music publishing company Ree and I started, now includes in its credits several awards and dozens of hits from the writers we represent.

In 1994 Arlene Sonday, the tutor who had helped my children become successful readers after they had struggled in school for years, asked me if our product development team could devise a way to bring her well-established teaching methods to a much broader audience. We formed Winsor Learning and now partner with school districts around the country to help their struggling readers succeed.

Did I develop all these enterprises by myself? Of course not. We all know that worthwhile success almost always involves many people. Yet looking back, I can see that I was the initiator who understood the uniqueness and market potential in each of these ideas, and I was also creatively involved in making them successful.

When I'm asked what I do for a living, I'm really not sure what to say. I'm fully aware that if I rattle off some of the things I do or have done, it comes across as unseemly boasting. So I usually change the subject. When I return from a trip outside the United States and fill out customs forms that ask for my occupation, I may respond with inventor or writer or designer or artist or chef. I'm not sure the US Customs Service is particular about what I do.

For my whole life, I've known that I'm not the smartest or cleverest person in any given room. And I don't light up that room when I walk into it. I have friends who do, and I like spending time with them. My dear friend Dick Byrd, who was a very successful team-building consultant for many Fortune 500 companies, used to tell me that he found the single most prevalent attribute of top-level executives was swagger. Swagger is not in my skill set, but I have recognized that I possess an ability to see what others often do not. I have led teams and cultivated ideas that have had significant success. But this hasn't always been the case.

I've come to understand that the insecurities of my youth were firmly established and reinforced by the educational systems I survived. My classmates always seemed smarter, quicker, and more knowledgeable about our class assignments than I was. It wasn't until I was 35 that I discovered why I bumped along the bottom of the academic riverbed: I had dyslexia. Discovering this fact as an adult did not magically make me feel smarter or more knowledgeable. But it has helped me understand how I developed the compensatory skills that have guided me in my various careers and in my relationships with other people over the years.

Following the encouragement of several friends, I decided to try to put together a book that could convey some of my concepts, and I'm extremely fortunate that Tim Walsh has chosen to work with me on this project. With his help, I've identified seven ideas that have helped me approach—and succeed at—a wide range of creative endeavors.

I'm sure that many others out there feel the way I used to—devoid of the skills needed to be productive and inventive. I'm completely convinced that we all—every one of us—have what it takes. I hope that in *Right Brain Red* you'll find one or two ideas that will help you reach your creative potential. And if you do, I will consider this book a very happy success.

Reyn Guyer
October 2015
Boca Grande, Florida

Idea #1

● ● ● ● ●

We *Is Greater than* Me*: The Power of a Great Team*

Jonathan Swift, author of *Gulliver's Travels*, wasn't an inventor. I'm willing to bet that if his words truly reflect his views, he would not have worked well in a team setting.

I'm sure we all recognize the image of the genius inventor concocting amazing new product ideas alone in his or her garage. There are many tales of inventors who have brought wonderful, life-changing new machines and products to the world. According to the legends built around these inventors, they've done it solo. I've never met one of these people.

I do know some folks who work alone on new ideas who say they don't want the deadweight of team members who don't produce. They'll admit to me that they've had a bad experience working in a team setting.

"If I want something done right, I'm the one I trust to get it right," they say.

I've met some who point to recent research that shows teams consistently underperform despite having more resources than individuals. I've read the research, too, and I contend that it's dysfunctional teams that underperform. I'll put my money on a good team anytime. And over the years, I have.

The team leaders I've been involved with are confident enough in their own abilities to allow others to contribute and shine. It's an approach that I've tried to emulate throughout my career. Show me

●●●●

> I'll put my money on a
> good team anytime.

a team that is passionate about a project and willing to share the leadership role among the whole group, and I'll show you a team that's about to accomplish something. Here are four ways of building great teams that have worked for me.

Clear Goals

We formed our educational company, Winsor Learning, with the intention of designing an educational product line that would help schools get struggling readers back on track. It all started with a remarkable woman who had a clear goal.

Arlene Sonday was a reading therapist when, in 1973, my wife, Mary, and I first asked her if she

---

●◦●●

Winsor Learning started with a remarkable woman who had a clear goal.

---

would work with our daughter Lisa. Lisa was diagnosed with dyslexia, a learning disability that alters the way the brain processes written material. As Mary and I began to understand the characteristics of this condition by observing Lisa, we soon recognized the same signs and symptoms in ourselves. This was a mixed blessing: The difficulties of dyslexia are real and substantial, but finally having a diagnosis helped us understand our own academic struggles over the years. We learned that dyslexia has a genetic component, so Mary and I were determined to help our kids escape the setbacks and negative labels that dyslexia had burdened us with during our school years.

Arlene tutored Lisa and, eventually, our other kids, Ree, Katie, Cindy, and Tom, as well. Arlene had trained in the Orton-Gillingham Approach (named after neuropsychiatrist Samuel Orton and educator and psychologist Anna Gillingham) to reading instruction, which uses a phonics-based, multisensory strategy. Her success in getting all our kids reading well was nothing short of amazing.

"Reyn, I know you know my methods work," she said to me one day. "Educators thank me all the time for helping their struggling readers, but I'm just one person, and I can't possibly work with all the students who need help. What happens if you and I work together to create a tutoring system that could train the average person to do what I do?"

It was a noble goal, but I wasn't sure that what she was suggesting was possible. Arlene Sonday had forgotten more about teaching students to read than most teachers would ever know. She had a master's degree in special education and had served as the first president of the Academy of Orton-Gillingham Practitioners and Educators. Teaching the average person to do what she did seemed impossible. But Arlene is an expert teacher, and she soon taught me something: Never doubt the power of a clear goal!

Someone once said, "Teamwork is the ability to work as a group toward a common vision, even if that vision becomes extremely blurry." The unknown author of that quote clearly understood one of the obstacles to reaching goals. The former sailor in me knows all too well how fast the fog can roll in and obscure where you're trying to go. There are almost always times when the goal that was so clear at the start of the project becomes fogbound and seemingly unattainable.

Losing clear sight of goals can—and usually does—happen at some point in any creative endeavor. When I'm in the middle of a painting,

---

Never doubt the power of a clear goal!

---

there always comes a moment when all seems lost. The spark that inspired me to begin the painting has vanished, and all I see on the canvas is a disorganized mess. Anyone who has chosen to undertake a creative project will readily admit to having experienced such moments, and they are real downers. We doubt our reason for starting, we doubt our ability to finish, and we doubt whether we have the experience to accomplish what our ambition led us to begin. In the end, we have all found, of course, that it is by pressing on through these moments that the project begins to come together. Somehow, we are able to step back, regain perspective, and renew the clear goals we started with.

When we released The Sonday System, I was certain we could emulate another seemingly successful reading system whose TV advertisements claimed that anyone who bought the product could learn to read. I was sure our product was better than theirs, so I convinced our team that making our own commercial would be the fastest way to get The Sonday System into the hands of the public and to turn a profit.

We created a fine TV commercial, collaborating with a group that was very experienced in direct-response TV advertising. We conducted a

There's always a moment when all seems lost. Pressing through these moments, we are able to renew the clear goals we started with.

test run of our commercial, and the results showed that it did not create enough consumer response to warrant a larger rollout. Suddenly our goal had met a very strong headwind. Fortunately, our team still believed that our product was the best on the market for helping struggling readers. So we pushed on the tiller of the Winsor Learning sailboat and reset our course.

I chose the sailboat metaphor for a reason. Starting when I was six years old, our family spent our summers on a lake near St. Paul, Minnesota. Sailboat racing was popular there, and most lake residents had a boat in front of their house. When I was nine, I found a set of sails under the Christmas tree. When I was thirteen, the aging, leaky hull of my first boat had to be replaced with a third-hand boat that didn't take on water faster than my crew and I could bail. With that boat, I began to win more than my share of races. I was happy to have my well-used but new-to-me boat, but I don't recall being aware of any reason for my new racing achievements. It was as if they just happened. It's only now, looking back, that I realize my sudden success was most likely due to the gift of intuition that comes with being dyslexic. The tactical part of sailing is essentially very intuitional. Overthinking the moves often leaves the skipper-tactician confused. I think I simply had a sense of the fluctuations of the wind and trusted that, when the wind shifted, I could respond by changing course and counting on it to shift back for me later.

We applied the same intuitive course correction to the Winsor Learning project. The goal for the project had not changed, but the course we charted to get there needed to change. Instead of trying to sell our system directly to consumers, we redesigned our business model to introduce our learning methods to school systems. It was an intuitive move. We trusted our product and we were aware that it would require more capital and more time. But, fortunately, our goal of giving struggling readers the gift of reading remained clear.

Effective Teamwork

When you are leading a creative group, teamwork means more than just being able to coexist with other people's ideas. I've found it indispensable to know the members of my team—how they work, what they're good at. When I know the team members well, I can combine them into effective groups in which the members' diverse skills complement each other.

I've also learned that a team is effective only if its size is manageable. Too few team members and your ideas may be limited; too many, and you risk having politics get in the way.

Knowing Your Team

When Arlene first approached me about creating a new product for the students who were struggling to learn to read, I took some time to consider who would be the person to work with Arlene on such a project. In the end, I chose my daughter Cindy. Since Cindy was once tutored by Arlene, she knew the material from the student's perspective. More importantly, Cindy has vast depths of patience. I knew patience would be crucial in helping Arlene work through the tedious task of writing out the entire system, lesson plan by lesson plan.

I also felt that Cindy's detail-oriented mind would be essential, and this, too, proved true. In the development process, we discovered that because Arlene knew the material so well, she had a tendency to skip instructional steps, jumping unawares, say, from step one to step five. Cindy slowed things down and coaxed steps two, three, and four from Arlene.

When you are leading a creative group, teamwork means more than just being able to coexist with other people's ideas.

It took Arlene and Cindy a year of intense effort, but, in the end, the results were amazing. They developed the first step-by-step program that gave an untrained tutor the tools to teach a struggling learner to read. Their work has become the model for The Sonday System and some of the subsequent training programs developed by Winsor Learning. It took a great team to make it happen. Great teams happen when the skills of each team member are complementary, not competitive.

* * *

Great teams are like great vocal harmonies. I've always had an innate ability to harmonize with others. I find the place where my voice fits, and I go there. When three or four people get together to sing, it's always good to know the various skills that each person brings to the group. The person singing lead must be able to hold the pitch while the others sing the various parts of the harmonies. At the same time, the harmonizers must know how to sing their part. Even an untrained ear can hear when a singing group has worked out each singer's role and the members trust each other to sing the parts correctly. When done right, it sounds mighty pretty. The analogy to team building is apt: The right team member in the right place can enhance a group. When it works, it's harmony.

I have one of those harmonious relationships with Jeff Harrington. In 1987, Jeff moved his family to Nashville so his kids could grow up in a neighborhood filled with young families, something Jeff and his wife couldn't seem to find in Los Angeles. Jeff is a versatile musician and songwriter who had already enjoyed several significant successes working with Scotti Brothers Records in LA. He settled into the Nashville music scene, writing for Warner Bros. Music.

About a year after he moved to Nashville, Jeff chose to join us at Wrensong publishing company.

Teams are like vocal harmonies. When done right, it's mighty pretty.

As Jeff and I got to know one another, we discovered that we had very similar musical tastes. We both loved children's music, and we became convinced we could write music for kids that also amused and challenged parents. The fantastical world of Curly Lasagna was born. Jeff wrote the music and acted as producer. I wrote the stories and songs and did all the voices, including the voice of Curly. We ended up with six cassette tapes for kids and parents to enjoy together. We called the project Curly Lasagna's Car Tapes. Our PBS affiliate in Minnesota liked Curly and partnered with us to pitch a Curly and Friends idea to the National Office of the Public Broadcasting System in Washington, DC. They liked the concept, but, in the end, chose instead to produce a show about a purple dinosaur.

Jeff and I were an effective team because our strengths were complementary. In areas where I was deficient, Jeff excelled, and vice versa. The wonderful thing about recognizing and admitting a blind spot in your own skill set is that you can seek out people who shine a light in that area and add them to your team. This allows teams to excel.

* * *

Our New-Age/Jazz project, *Lyrias*, took shape when Jeff took some poetry I had written and set it to music. Then we started thinking that our skills could combine to create compelling pop music for theater. Once we set our sights on writing a musical for the stage, we really had fun. We created a ninety-minute musical drama with a four-person cast entitled *Stained Glass*. We're being told it's a powerful piece of theater. So far, the show has had three runs, and we're working on booking it into medium and small theaters around the country.

As a two-person team, Jeff and I have developed a method of working together that is quite effective. It's not that we don't have intense disagreements about the direction a project may take—we certainly do! But when we do disagree, we respect each other's point of view. I think that's because neither of us is absolutely sure that we're right! I know Jeff's music chops are truly professional and mine aren't, while Jeff continues to respect my approach to the written word.

* * *

Respect for each team member's strengths and acknowledgment of what each member brings to the team are critical, especially in the afterglow of a success. I once put together a team around one of my ideas, and we had huge success, but it turned out that I didn't know the personalities of the group members as well as I thought I did. I had hired Chuck Foley to help further develop an idea for a mat game that I had when I was working in the design firm my father and I owned. Chuck was a sharp guy, but I discovered the hard way that he wasn't a team player. After he and I—and my entire team—developed the game that would eventually become the mega-hit Twister, Chuck walked into my office and announced he was quitting. It turns out that he had found a backer and was opening up his own game design firm to compete with us and taking one of our best artists with him. I thought I knew my team, but I did not. The hard truth is some people don't play well with others. Critically judging the personalities of your team members is crucial.

Committees

Teams work, but bigger has not always necessarily been better for me. Teams of two can be very effective if the team members have complementary skill sets. Teams of three are often the most effective and innovative. But with teams of three, there is a real danger of having one member become the odd man out. In my experience, teams of four or five can achieve great things but may require more time to get there. Teams of six or more, I've found, aren't teams—they're committees.

In my experience, the level of success achieved when large numbers of people—even very competent, thoughtful people—come together to make decisions is disappointing at best. I've endured memberships on boards of hospitals, boards of

Teams work, but bigger is not always better.

trustees, and church vestries, and I've found the operative phrase for the experiences is, I regret to say, sleep inducing. The following excerpt from a poem I wrote tells you how I feel about committees!

Find a twenty-foot table
And forty-odd chairs
And eighteen odd people,
Or thirty—who cares?

Then call in a chairman,
A man worth his weight,
Who rows a tight rowboat
And never comes late.

And with all those good people
And adequate votes
And minutes of minutes
And boxes of notes,

If there's ever an issue,
If there's ever some doubt,
Just start a committee
To check it all out.

Find a fourteen-foot table
And twenty-odd chairs
And seven odd people,
Or nineteen—who cares?

Then call up somebody
To see if she'll be
The under-vice-chair
Whenever she's free

And with a full quorum
And just enough votes
And two minutes of minutes
And one page of notes,

You'll know that in spite of
What some people claim,
There's no one, but no one,
But no one to blame.

In my experience, teams of from two to five members seem to have the best chance of playing (and working) together. Larger than that, and your group gets unwieldy. It's all about harmony. So form a great team and go make beautiful music together.

Passion

My son, Tom, was another of Arlene's success stories. When The Sonday System was finally ready to be introduced, Tom was a passionate believer, if not an eager salesman.

"I was reluctant to go out there and sell, because

I am not a natural salesman," he said. "But then I realized that I had a great story, so that's what I focused on. I didn't sell the system; I just told the truth: I was that struggling kid who got connected to a great tutor with a proven method, and now she's our author, and I'm the president of the company! To this day, that is my sales pitch. I simply tell the truth with passion."

Passion is contagious. "The best people on my team are former educators who have used The Sonday System," says Tom. "They're people who come to us and say, 'This is the best program I've ever seen. I'm getting great results with my students, but I want to do more. I want to come work for you!'"

Passion is contagious.

Tom told me about a woman who was once a turnaround principal in some of the toughest schools in South Carolina. In one particular school, it wasn't that seventy-eight kids were failing—it was more like 78 percent of the kids were failing. She installed The Sonday System and turned that school around in eighteen months. After that, she went to work for the state of South Carolina as a turnaround specialist, and then she came to work for us.

She's not a sales person; she's an ambassador. She really believes in the product, the system, the whole idea, and her obvious passion and enthusiasm translate into purpose and an intriguing pitch. It's not difficult to understand why passionate people are the most productive people.

Thinking Big

Our goal at Winsor Learning is to help schools get kids who are behind in their reading skills back on track. But everyone in our organization is aware that we are working toward something bigger. Struggling to read starts as a small setback, but it can quickly spiral into low self-esteem, misguided beliefs regarding intelligence, judgment from peers, and so on. So yes, we're giving tutors a system to improve the reading skill of their students. But what we're really doing is empowering tutors to change the lives of students for the better. Since 1997, The Sonday System has helped over 1,800 school districts get struggling readers back on track and has improved the lives of over 500,000 students.

* * *

So, at Winsor Learning we are all aware that we contribute meaningfully to the lives of every person to

What we're really doing is empowering tutors to change the lives of students for the better.

whom we give the gift of reading. That doesn't mean that I always take my own advice and think big. In the early 1980s, Charlie Girsch encouraged me to put together a new team of toy and game developers with him as head of sales. Charlie was a former priest with whom I had worked on some community issues and who, to this day, remains one of the most natural-born salesmen I've ever met. The team of designers I put together was really promising. Each member would go on to have success in various toy and game development companies around the country. Ed Hollihan was one such designer.

Ed was the youngest member of the team and definitely had his ear to the ground when it came to new trends. During one of our Monday meetings, Ed shared his perception that trivia was gaining in popularity. So we charged him to come up with a game in which players would challenge each other to respond to trivia questions. The prototype game Ed developed tested really well, but the estimated cost to produce it was discouraging. The game would need so many cards that the retail price would be three times the accepted industry norm for a board game. And then there was the even greater problem that once people played the game a few times, they would easily memorize the questions and answers. So we passed on further developing Ed's idea.

Too bad for us. Trivial Pursuit, the smash-hit game, sold twenty million copies when it debuted in the US in 1984. There's a strong chance we had missed out on a fantastic opportunity by not thinking big enough.

* * *

When it comes time to put together a team, I keep these four tenets in mind:

- build a team with clear goals
- choose partners who work well together
- bring passion to the project
- think big

They've often worked for me.

Idea #2

● ● ● ●

What Happens if . . .

"Who questions much, shall learn much, and retain much."
—Francis Bacon

In "Ali Baba and the Forty Thieves," a poor wood-cutter discovers that speaking the words *Open sesame!* magically opens a sealed cave filled with gold. If only unlocking the magic concepts available to your team in an idea session were that easy: *Open sesame!, Abracadabra!,* or *Alakazam!* probably won't get you the gold you're looking for, but I have found three other magic words that just might.

As naive and simplistic as it sounds, the three little words *what happens if* have served as one of the most useful tools I've found for encouraging creative thinking and sharing in a team setting. We're all aware of the many phrases that discourage the give-and-take of a team. *I want to, My idea is to,* and *I think we should* are well-known collaboration killers. Likewise, *ought to* and *should* can also kill a creative dialogue.

When I explain the usefulness of these three magic words, *what happens if*, often someone points out that the words *what if* can be just as useful and lead to the same results. Well, they don't. They are almost as useful, but just not specific enough.

What if we launch this product? does not generate specific answers the way that *What happens if we launch this product?* does. Posing the question with *what happens if* immediately asks us to consider the details that might lead to asking the question in the first place. It further prompts us to look more broadly at the picture of what happens before, during, and after the launch of the product in question.

What happens if will lead a group to consider the many important details of the problem that is posed. Below, I point out some notable instances when the three magic words have been very effective for me.

What Happens if Is Playful

What happens if seeks the participation of others. It invites answers and, in so doing, prompts collaboration and a feeling of playfulness.

As I mentioned in the previous chapter, Arlene Sonday is a world-renowned educator who works with our company, Winsor Learning. One day I was chatting with Arlene about the alphabet song, which has been around for 180 years. Arlene was describing how the song can be confusing to early readers because it mashes together the letters L, M, N, O, and P so that they sound like "elemenopee."

------●●●●------

What happens if prompts collaboration and a feeling of playfulness.

I asked her, "What happens if I try to write a new alphabet tune that doesn't scramble those letters together?"

Arlene told me to go for it, and I did. Now my new alphabet song is part of Winsor Learning's "Let's Play Learn" program for early readers. It's playful, and I had fun writing it.

What Happens if Gives Us Permission to Do What We Do Best

What happens if offers possibility instead of impos-ing unintentional limits. When all the members of a group realize that they are all being asked to con-tribute, a sense of camaraderie often grows as they all interact. I love to watch those moments.

A few years ago, I was attending an annual meeting of the Gasparilla Island Conservation and Improvement Association. Over the years, this organization has worked on behalf of the residents of Gasparilla Island, a small barrier island on the southwest coast of Florida, where we live. At the meeting, the president mentioned that an island landowner was interested in making his seventy acres available to the conservancy for a reasonable price.

After the meeting, I asked the president, "What happens if I pull together a small group of my friends to discuss raising the money needed to con-serve that land?"

What happens if offers possibility
instead of imposing limits.

He enthusiastically supported my inquiry.

I called a bunch of friends who were all successful in their business careers. I was careful to choose people who I felt had a specific skill they could bring to a fund-raising project.

At our first meeting as a group, I opened the discussion by asking, "What happens if we organize a campaign to raise the money needed to purchase the land?"

From there, the skills of each of member of the team emerged because the team members had permission to do what they could do best. The organizers organized, the fund-raisers raised funds, and my friend John Hillenbrand II, who was familiar with the nuances of conservancy, worked with the Gasparilla Island Conservation and Improvement Association's president to purchase the land from the seller. The leadership of the project remained with the president and, in the end, our team of friends raised almost a million dollars more than the purchase price and provided an endowment to care for the land for future generations.

I firmly believe that if I had said, "I want to write a song to replace the alphabet song," or "I want to raise three million dollars to conserve this land," people would have resisted, maybe even thought I was crazy. By broaching the seemingly impossible with *what happens if*, we give people permission to dream big. It's powerful.

Benjamin E. Mays, the minister, businessman, educator, and social activist, once said, "It must be borne in mind that the tragedy of life doesn't lie in not reaching your goal. The tragedy lies in having no goals to reach. Not failure, but low aim is sin."

●-●-●-●

> By broaching the seemingly impossible with *what happens if* we give people permission to dream big.

What Happens if Fosters Openness

Please don't think these magic words express some naively optimistic, *kumbaya* philosophy. Not all ideas are good, and I don't buy into the brainstorming creed of never expressing a negative opinion. On the contrary, my experience is that when team members find they are free to express their opinions, both positive and negative, with no limits, a sense of respect enters into the deliberations. Over the years, I've gotten into a habit of using *what*

"The department budget cut back on breathalyzers. Left foot yellow."

happens if when testing an idea's legitimacy, and it almost always brings a positive spin to what might be a negative discussion. *What happens if we can't reach that price point? What happens if the consumer misses the point?* Openness often leads to answers.

In Idea #6: Be Open, we explore the important benefits of this concept in greater depth.

What Happens if Sparks Curiosity

This is perhaps the most subtle yet powerful result of using these three magic words. As leaders of meetings and minds, our job is to foster creativity in our teams and ourselves. A catalyst to creativity is curiosity. I'm a big fan of curiosity; if it hadn't killed the cat, she might have died of boredom.

The most interesting people I know are curious. They ask questions and look into new things. We all start off this way. Curiosity is what makes us reach for something and then later crawl toward something else. Curiosity leads us to mimic sounds and eventually find our voice. But over time, it's easy to lose this marvelous trait. If we stop asking questions, we risk thinking in limiting ways or—worse yet—not thinking at all. *What happens if* stimulates us to stay curious.

What Happens if Teaches Us to Be Fearless

The more present we are, the more we set aside worries and cares about the future. I credit Richard E. Byrd, author of *A Guide to Personal Risk Taking*,[1] for guiding me to this philosophy: "In the beginning God created constant change. Change accompanies health, vocation, maturing, reorganization, relationships, bus schedules, technologies—all in all, our entire social fabric. Change is the way to

---

1 Byrd, Richard E. *A Guide to Personal Risk Taking.* New York: AMACOM, 1978.

describe the nature of the day. With it come risk and continual uncertainty."

Dick was fearless in the face of change. He was an Episcopal minister, a pioneer in the area of personal and organizational development, a consultant to Fortune 500 companies, and a great personal friend. He'd say things like, "God made us with two ears and one mouth, so I think he wants us to listen twice as much as we talk."

His most cherished ideal was "be in the moment." I've never met a more positive person. Worry and anxiety wanted nothing to do with him. Another friend told me the story of his attempt to needle Dick during a plane ride.

"Okay, Dick," our friend said. "What happens if that window breaks and you get sucked out of this plane right now? What would you do then?"

Without even thinking about it, Dick said, "I'd probably stretch out my arms and attempt to fly at first. After that, if I had time, I might move on to try some somersaults."

What happens if is a form of creative risk taking, because the question implies an openness to change. As humans, we all understand that a certain degree of wariness about change is probably good, but a chronic fear of change is limiting and can even be self-destructive.

I'm willing to bet that every one of us has a friend stuck in a job they don't find stimulating. Yet for some reason, they refuse to allow themselves to look for a career that could excite them. I'm no counselor, but I suspect these people have a serious fear of change and, for them, staying in a familiar situation seems safer than the unknown. Perhaps asking themselves, *what happens if* could help them face their fear and eventually find the courage to make a change.

What Happens if Leads to New Ideas

Over the years, *what happens if* has become a habit with me. When I'm alone with my thoughts, I often revisit old ideas, and the reflexive use of those three words will, on occasion, shine a new light on old subjects.

A few months ago, just before I was heading out on a two-week vacation, I impulsively pulled down some CDs that Jeff Harrington and I had written, produced, marketed, and then abandoned more than twenty years ago. I figured that I would have time on my hands on my vacation, so in the late afternoons, I would sit back and listen to the collection of stories and songs called Curly Lasagna that Jeff Harrington and I had created for children and their parents. Then one morning, as I was slowly waking up, I began to reflect on the fact that, over the past twenty-five years, the marketplace had dramatically changed.

(Yup, here it comes, folks.)

I asked myself, "What happens if we restyle and reintroduce the material for the digital outlets that are now available to us?" In addition to what has historically been a vast, highly regimented network of retail outlets, an array of online music sources has emerged that act like digital retailers. These places could sell our product by the story, song, or CD! And then, wow! "What happens if Curly Lasagna has his own website?" I can happily report that Curly not only has his own website now, but is also enjoying a very successful, revitalized career.

What happens if is an open invitation to possibilities.

Four albums of Curly Lasagna stories and songs.

The process of creating new music is almost always joyful for me. There's no place on earth more fun than a recording studio, and musicians are some of the funniest people alive. *What happens if* is an open note and an open invitation to possibilities.

In 1985, when my daughter Ree and I were starting up Wrensong Music in Nashville, a Minnesota songwriter named John Kurhajetz wrote a song called "Gonna Take a Lot of River." Ree and I knew it was a winner, but we also recognized that the song needed a small middle section known as a bridge. John struggled to write a bridge, so we threw the puzzle out to some of our other songwriters. One morning, Mark Henley walked in with the perfect bridge that tied the whole song together. All Mark did was ask, "What happens if the song becomes a story?" It became one of Wrensong's early successes and a number-one *Billboard* country hit for the Oak Ridge Boys.

Below are the lyrics for "Gonna Take a Lot of River," with the bridge in italics to illustrate how adding some narrative about the woman who was probably the source of the singer's blues turned the song into a story—a simple but very effective embellishment.

> I ain't gonna ride no rail or hitchhike down
> no highway.
> I ain't going nowhere feeling the way I do.
> Because my baby's long gone and nothing's
> going my way.
> I'm gonna let this muddy water just wash
> away my blues.
>
> It's gonna take a lot of river,
> To keep this broken heart afloat.
> Gonna take a lot of river,
> Running all the livelong day.
> Gonna take the Mississippi, the
> Monongahela, and the Ohio.
> Gonna take a lot of river
> To wash these blues away.

Well, I wish I was tugboat pushing and
pulling them barges along,
Moving on the water with a heart made of
iron and steel.
There wouldn't be no women who could ever
take my loving and do me wrong.
I could work all day with nothing in the world
to feel.

It's gonna take a lot of river,
To keep this broken heart afloat.
Gonna take a lot of river,
Running all the livelong day.
Gonna take the Mississippi, the
Monongahela, and the Ohio.
Gonna take a lot of river
To wash these blues away.

Is she in New Orleans?
Is she a Cajun queen?
I wonder what she's doing now.
But if I know her, she's got rings and furs,
Struggling along somehow,
Struggling along somehow.

It's gonna take a lot of river,
To keep this broken heart afloat.
Gonna take a lot of river,

Running all the livelong day.
Gonna take the Mississippi, the
Monongahela, and the Ohio.
Gonna take a lot of river
To wash these blues away.
It's gonna take a lot of river
To wash these blues away.

John Kurhajetz and Mark Henley with Ree
at the ASCAP Awards in 1989.

Whether I'm opening a group planning session or just dreaming on my own, it's become my habit start off with my three magic words: *what happens if.*

I encourage everyone to give them a try. As a song-writer, I understand the power of just the right words, and these three are music to my ears.

Idea #3

● ● ● ● ●

Break a Rule

"Hell, there are no rules here—
we are trying to accomplish something."
—Thomas Alva Edison

Oliver Wendell Holmes Sr. once said, "The young man knows the rules, but the old man knows the exceptions." I agree. As a young man working for my father's design company in St. Paul, Minnesota, I knew that our main job was to make in-store point-of-purchase (POP) displays that drew attention to our Fortune 500 clients' products. Our client list included Kraft Foods, Pillsbury, 3M, Brach Candies, S.C. Johnson Wax, and others. Our displays may have been clever (my father held over 120 patents in paper-carton packaging design), but to me, they weren't the future. Whenever my entrepreneurial spirit pulled me in a new direction, my father would listen patiently and quietly and then remind me that the primary rule at the Reynolds Guyer Agency of Design was "POP displays pay the bills."

Some of the in-store displays made by the Reynolds Guyer Agency of Design.

I understood my dad's rule, but I felt increasingly boxed in. I even began to experience what I thought was a fear of flying whenever I headed off to Chicago, Cincinnati, or St. Louis to cultivate new clients. In time, I realized that flying on planes for vacations didn't make me anxious at all, so I put that assumed phobia aside.

One day, after returning from yet another anxiety-inducing business trip, I went into my dad's office and confessed to him that if we didn't start looking for a new path to take the business, I might have to look for another way to make a living. I shared my concern that our business model could never generate long-term growth if we continued working order to order with no possibility for residual income. To his credit, my father recognized that there are always exceptions to the rules. I don't remember a time when he discouraged me from trying something new.

There are always exceptions to the rules.

* * *

One of my wilder rule-breaking ideas was a project called Pizza in the Round, which I dreamed up in 1960. I worked on it in my spare time so I wouldn't tie up any of our company's funds or time on the project. I got pretty far down the line before I realized that the next step would require far more capital and expertise than I or my potential partners possessed.

The idea behind Pizza in the Round was to have customers drive up to a window at one end of a building where they would order and pay, and then just a minute later, drive away from the other end of the building with a pizza topped just the way they liked it. All of this would be achieved by using the totally new Radarange oven (i.e., a microwave) and a frozen pizza crust.

I entreated a prominent young architect in the Twin Cities to design the building, and he came up with a really cool Venetian look, with thin red-and-white-striped barber poles as the support girders. The idea hit snags when I discovered that the one Radarange in the metropolitan area was in the cafeteria of the Minneapolis newspaper building, and the only place I could find that frozen pizza crust was at a small bar in West St. Paul. I managed to conduct a couple of tests of the concept in the cafeteria's Radarange and they only emphasized my culinary incompetence. I've often thought how fortunate I was to realize early enough that I lacked knowledge of the franchise food industry. It surely kept me from chasing the concept to completion and, most likely, from suffering an early fiscal failure.

On the other hand, if I had found a way to succeed with the concept, we would have broken the rule that pizza has to bake in an oven for at least twenty minutes before it reaches the customer. We would have been able to deliver the pizza in pretty close to a minute.

Reaching out in search of new ideas is a mysterious process. We never know when and where the magic moment might happen. Sometimes we strike gold when we're mining far from where we started. And sometimes we find treasure when we're digging close to home.

* * *

Fast forward to 1964. I was dreaming up a mail-in offer for a brand of shoe polish made by one of our biggest customers, S.C. Johnson Wax. I wondered what would happen if consumers could mail in a dollar and a box top from a shoe polish package, and in return receive a game to play in their living rooms. Since the promotion involved shoes, I envisioned a mat game played on the floor. The mat could have squares, like a giant game board, that kids would step on as they played. Suddenly I was aware that the concept held greater possibilities. As far as I knew, there were no games on the market in which the players acted as the game pieces on a giant board.

I went to the design department, pulled out a large sheet of cardboard, and drew 24 one-foot squares in a four-by-six arrangement. Next I put out a call for testers within our own offices and had no trouble getting a group of people eager to play. Even our very pregnant receptionist was game. Eight of us stood on the mat, and I divided us into teams by color—green, red, blue, and yellow. As I remember, I instructed each team to try to be first to reach the square on the board that was diagonally opposite from the corner where they started. They could accomplish this by moving to an adjacent square on their turn. It quickly became clear that the exact rules didn't make any difference because we were laughing so hard. If we're trying to define the "aha" moment for the idea, this was it. It didn't make any difference that the game we were playing wasn't a "real" game—we were having too much fun to care!

The real magic of the game
that would become Twister was
that it gave players permission
to break a social rule.

A sketch of my recollection of my very first try at making
a "people are the game pieces" game.

The game was a riot, and I immediately knew it was more than a promotion for shoe polish. Somewhere in the giggles, we were all enjoying the makings of a retail product. On a more analytical level, I recognized that the real magic of the game that would become Twister was that it gave players permission to break the social rule of respecting other people's personal space, and that created fun! And not just smiling fun—belly-busting, laugh-out-loud fun!

I jumped into my next task, which was to come up with a real game, played on a mat on the floor, that had winners and losers. I designed the mat as a five-by-five grid of squares. One team of two players wore red bands wrapped around each of their ankles, and the other team of two wore blue bands. The first team to get all four of their ankle bands in a row won the game. I called the game King's Footsie.

I took a prototype of the game to our client, 3M—known today for its office products, but in the 1960s it had a successful line of games. King's Footsie really didn't fit 3M's more reserved brand of table-top games, and they passed on it. It became apparent that changing the course of our company would not be easy. I needed a team.

One day Chuck Foley, a salesman for a silk-screen printing company, was soliciting business from Phil Shaber, our purchasing agent. Chuck saw the prototype of the King's Footsie game and asked about it. Phil told Chuck it was a game I had developed, and Chuck mentioned that he had experience in the toy and game industry. So I met with Chuck and learned that he had once worked for Lakeside Toys in Minneapolis. I explained my idea of having a mat game played on the floor in which people act as the game pieces, and Chuck recognized the uniqueness of the idea. He suggested we hire him and a friend of his named Neil Rabens, an artist who had experience working for a children's pool-toy company, to further develop the idea.

So I went to my dad and outlined a new direction

our company could take, where I could lead a team consisting of Foley, Rabens, and myself. My dad fully understood the possibilities of the game because he had witnessed the fun we had had play-testing it. Never one to tiptoe into anything, my dad went to the bank and got us two years' worth of funding. With his commitment, the Reynolds Guyer Agency of Design stepped boldly into the business of fun.

In 1965, I hired Chuck and Neil, and we set out to take the "players are the game pieces" idea further. As a team, we seemed to synchronize well. Ultimately, we invented eight games, for four-year-olds up to young adults. King's Footsie was still a standout. But the new idea we were most excited about involved having the players step on red, yellow, green, or blue circles. Chuck suggested organizing the mat so that the four colors lined up in rows of six circles. This change was a big improvement and became a part of the patent application. A few days later, Neil made the key suggestion that the players use their hands as well as their feet. We knew that this wrinkle was a drastic one, but, wow, did it ever increase the fun! This too became part of the patent application. We added a spinner divided into four quadrants, each containing the four colors of the mat and a specific hand or foot (left foot, right foot, left hand, right hand). The needle would land on a specific color and body part, and we'd call out "left foot blue!" or "right hand red!" and hilarity would ensue. We called the game Pretzel, "the game that ties you up in knots."

Chuck and I took the eight games we had developed to Milton Bradley, where we met with Mel Taft, senior vice president of research and development. Mel had never seen mat games played on the floor. He liked them immediately and singled out Pretzel as a winner. Other executives at Milton Bradley were not so sure. They warned Mel that the idea of being that close to someone—especially someone of the opposite sex—was socially unacceptable. The rule we were breaking almost broke the deal. Thankfully, Mel Taft was a rule breaker, too.

"I was getting so much flack in-house that I took the thing home," Mel recalled. "We had three other couples over and as soon as we started, I got to laughing so hard that I damn-near had appendicitis. I knew this thing was worth its weight in gold. . . . If adults could have that much fun . . . somehow, we had to get it in the hands of consumers."

If the internal resistance Mel was facing weren't enough, Milton Bradley's lawyers found a toy dog named Pretzel produced by a competitor, which meant that the name of our game had to change. When Mel told me Milton Bradley had settled on Twister, I was not pleased. Having grown up in the Midwest, where twisters appear suddenly out of storm clouds and kill people, I thought the new name was a terrible choice. But in the end, I figured we were breaking other rules, so why not name the game Twister? Little did I know, the perfect storm was gathering.

In 1966, Milton Bradley's sales team showed Twister to some key retailers prior to the annual Toy Fair convention, the US toy industry's major trade show. The buyers balked. I got a call from Mel, who told me that the Sears buyer had proclaimed the game "too risqué" and said Sears would not stock it. Sears was so powerful back then that its decision could make or break a product. Twister was dead.

But then someone with more power than Sears gave the game a spin. Even though the game was "dead," Mel had already paid a public relations company to promote it. On May 3, 1966, the PR company somehow got Twister into the hands of the folks who ran *The Tonight Show*. Johnny Carson was the host at that time, and it was a lucky break that his guest that night was the actress and socialite Eva Gabor. Watching the King of Late Night and his refined, elegantly dressed guest on all fours on the Twister mat sent America into hysterics and, the next day, straight into stores in search of the game. And what do you know? Sears reconsidered. Over three million games were sold in 1967, and the rule-breaking game that "ties you up in knots" hasn't slowed down since.

The Tonight Show on May 3, 1966,
with Johnny Carson and Eva Gabor.

Two years after Twister was released, my team's second rule-breaking toy became a hit. The NERF ball broke the ever-present family rule, "Thou shall not play ball in the house!" And it did so without breaking lamps or windows! The whole story of NERF appears in Idea #4: Look Outside.

There are, of course, many other examples of successful ideas that fly in the face of conformity. The toy industry is rife with rule breakers.

Some toys broke family rules:

"Don't play with your food!" (Mr. Potato Head)

Some broke industry rules:

"You can't sell a board game for more than $20."
(Trivial Pursuit)
"Puzzles can't be difficult to solve, or they won't sell."
(Rubik's Cube)

Some broke societal rules:

"Boys will never play with a doll!" (G.I. Joe)
"Girls only want baby dolls so they can pretend
to be a mom." (Barbie)

No matter what business or industry we're in, there are always patterns, habits, rules, or rituals that define and instruct what we do on a daily basis. Keeping an eye out for new ideas, products, practices, or services that break from tradition and could transform a business is always a good idea.

* * *

In 1987, I bought a building on 17th Avenue in Nashville, part of the area known as Music Row. Like almost all the buildings on 16th and 17th Avenues, the building was originally a family home. My daughter Ree and I renovated the first floor into our office space for Wrensong Music, the publishing company we had started. We decided to keep the second floor as rental space for the two women who lived there. One of those women, Kathy, was a singer whose career was about to take off.

Kathy often spent time in our coffee room with some of our songwriters, one of whom was Jon Vezner. One day, Kathy's car died in the parking lot. Jon, a Minnesota native who knew how to jump-start a car and had the cables to prove it, offered his help. And that was the start of a legendary Music Row romance.

After they were married, Jon wrote a song called "Where've You Been?" about his grandparents visiting each other from separate rooms in the same hospital. Kathy decided to put the song on her new album. Ree spent a lot of time and effort trying to convince Kathy's record label to make the song a single. It was a new kind of song that told a story progressively, in three verses. Time and time again Ree was told, "Radio stations will never play a four-minute song. It's too long!"

Thank goodness Ree stuck to her guns and convinced the record label to break that rule, because "Where've You Been" went on to be a top-ten hit for Kathy Mattea and won the CMA and ACM awards for Best Country Song of the Year in 1990. The song broke a rule and won a Grammy in the process.

Left to right—Reyn, Mary, Kathy Mattea, Jon Vezner, and Ree.

* * *

According to William Taylor and Polly LaBarre in *Mavericks at Work: Why the Most Original Minds in Business Win*,[2]

2   Taylor, William C., and Polly LaBarre. *Mavericks at Work: Why the Most Original Minds in Business Win.* New York: William Morrow, 2006.

When it comes to thriving in a hypercompeti-
tive marketplace, "playing it safe" is no longer
playing it smart. [And, in business,] mavericks do the work that matters most—the work
of originality, creativity, and experimenta-
tion. . . . Business, at its best, is too exciting,
too important, and too much fun to be left to
the dead hand of business as usual.

Imagine how different the business landscape
would look if Amazon's Jeff Bezos had bought into
the belief that no one would buy books on the Inter-
net. How would the entertainment world look today
if Orson Welles had accepted the dictum that "you
can't cowrite, produce, direct, and star in your own
film"? What if Ray Charles believed he couldn't own
his own song masters or if the creatives at HBO
believed they couldn't produce their own original
content? Rule breakers, one and all.

●◦●◦●

Imagine if Amazon's Jeff Bezos had bought into the belief that no one would buy books on the Internet.

It's been nearly fifty years since a broken rule led me to a very enjoyable success with Twister. I've kept my eyes open for that kind of opportunity ever since. To this day, when I hear resistance to an idea, I get excited. Experience tells me I just might be onto something. In meetings, at power lunches, and during brainstorming sessions, I'm especially attuned to words like *never*, *always*, *can't*, *won't*, and *don't*. They seem to set off an internal alarm in me—it's like a metal detector alerting me to pay attention. Somewhere in those words may lie hidden treasure where another hard-and-fast rule is waiting to be broken.

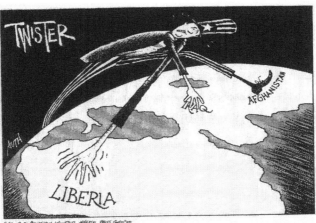

Idea #4

● ● ● ●

Look Outside

"An object in motion tends to remain in motion along a
straight line unless acted upon by an outside force."
—Sir Isaac Newton

I once had a friend scold me: "Stop poking your
nose into businesses that you have no experience in," he said pointedly. "Concentrate on one
thing!" His unsolicited advice killed our friend-
ship. Maybe he had diagnosed me with attention
deficit disorder (he was not a doctor), or perhaps
he looked at my reasoned ventures as haphazard
plunges into the unknown (he was not an entrepreneur). Looking back, I think it was his own
fear of uncertainty that bothered him. I know one
thing for sure: My old friend underestimated the
power of looking outside.

In his groundbreaking book, *Borrowing Brilliance*,[3] David Kord Murray describes how when Johannes Gutenberg invented the printing press, believed by many to be the most important invention in human history, he borrowed a gear from screw presses used by winemakers and olive-oil producers. Murray also describes how Henry Ford found inspiration in Chicago's meatpacking companies, which moved meat on hooks along a conveyor system. Ford reversed the idea—from taking something apart to putting something together—to create the modern assembly line. Looking outside helped Gutenberg educate the world and turned Ford into a titan of business.

As if these examples weren't impressive enough, medical breakthroughs that could save the human race are coming from outside the field of medicine. At the University of Washington, research scientists had been trying to figure out the exact structure of a very complicated AIDS-like virus for fifteen years. Faced with a dead end, in 2008 the scientists at UW did something bold. They looked outside and created a collaborative online game portal called FOLDIT. There, puzzle enthusiasts and game geeks could work together using a 3D modeling game to try to map the structure of the virus that had eluded

---

3   Murray, David Kord. *Borrowing Brilliance: The Six Steps to Business Innovation by Building on the Ideas of Others*. New York: Gotham Books, 2009.

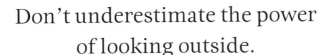

Don't underestimate the power of looking outside.

the scientists. As a test, the scientists planned to keep FOLDIT active for three weeks and then see if anyone had come close to an answer. A group of game players solved the fifteen-year-old problem in fewer than ten days.

According to the article published in the journal *Nature Structural & Molecular Biology*, most of the players on the winning team had "little or no background in biochemistry."[4] But before we give too much credit to the gamers, recognize the genius and humility of the researchers who developed the FOLDIT game. They had the vision to call on outsiders to help, and their hunch was right. Sometimes, fresh eyes and a different skill set can create breakthroughs. Using tools or materials that aren't normally a part of our field may allow us to solve a big problem or uncover dormant opportunities.

* * *

4 Khatib, Firas, et al. "Crystal Structure of a Monomeric Retroviral Protease Solved by Protein Folding Game Players." *Nature Structural & Molecular Biology* 18 (2011): 1175–1177.

By 1968, my father and I were co-owners of the in-store display business he had begun in 1956. As I described in the previous chapter, my disenchantment with the company's business model was a large part of what led us to the development of Twister and the surprise success that followed. I wanted to continue in this new direction and develop more toys and games, so I struck a deal with my father that gave him the entire display business and half of the proceeds from the Twister royalties. Looking back, I am grateful that my father was open to looking outside.

I assembled a new team of five people and chose to call the enterprise Winsor Concepts. The building that I had found for the display business four years before had far more empty space than it could dream of using. So I chose to rent some of the unused space and build an office and workspace adjacent to the display business.

One room was octagonal, with rough-cedar walls and a carpet to deaden sound. It had a card table and six chairs for playing new board game inventions. It also had seating around a coffee table, with a sofa and matching chairs for casual meetings.

In the adjacent room, each of the five of us had workstations and drawing boards that were placed in a large circle, and we all faced the middle of the room. My hope was that this arrangement might encourage give-and-take and involvement in each other's projects. In retrospect, I think it had a very positive effect on encouraging us to be supportive of each other's undertakings. There was a third room filled with lathes, drills, saws, and tool benches. Beyond that workroom, we had access to a wide open area for a variety of play testing.

The team members I chose came from a variety of disciplines. Norton Cross was an acquaintance who I knew was always coming up with ideas, none of which had yet found a home. Norton also served as our head of sales, whom I would step in to support when necessary. This arrangement also allowed me to be more focused on product development and not in constant contact with toy and game companies. Marty Lundquist came with me from my father's company, as did Kenny Barnes. Each of them felt that toy and game development would be more exciting than the display business. Marty became a fine model maker, and Ken was an excellent product illustrator. The fifth team member, Will Kruse, came aboard after Marty suggested that his creativity could benefit us.

Every Monday morning, the team would meet to plan the allocation of projects and responsibilities for the coming week. Each project had a leader who was responsible for coordinating the use of each team member's skills to create and test the ideas that were essential to the project. At least once a week, teams of two or three would head out to one or two stores that sold toys and games with the purpose of staying current with what was happening at the retail level.

In our first eight months of operation, Winsor Concepts had not developed any significant new concepts to show for our efforts. One day, Norton Cross scheduled an afternoon testing of a caveman game he had been developing. It was another "players are the game pieces" concept, where kids would walk around on small sheets of plastic painted to look like stepping-stones. Each player had some coins, which they could keep or hide under a stepping-stone, and two gray foam "rocks." The players threw the foam rocks at their opponents to stop them from stealing coins from under the stepping-stones.

It was definitely not a great game, and, try as we might, we couldn't figure out a way to save it. The spirit of our testing program was that no matter how doubtful an idea appeared to be, we would give it a try. I strongly encouraged team members to withhold judgment on a new project prior to testing it because I hoped that something unusual might jump out at us from virtually nowhere. On this afternoon, with that spirit in mind, it happened.

As the caveman game disintegrated, Will Kruse took a couple of the foam rocks and started tossing them around. Soon, an all-out battle ensued as we pelted each other with the rocks. As the laughter faded, we all realized that something exciting had happened. There we were, five supposedly grown-up guys, hurling chunks of lightweight foam at each other, and no one was hurt. We had inadvertently created the world's first indoor ball!

Our next move was to acquire all sorts of different densities of foam and cut them into different sizes of balls. We had broken the parental rule "no throwing balls in the house" and had done so by looking outside our expectations to find a new and unique application of a known material. After some digging, we found distributors of the foam material, which was essentially used as padding for shipping delicate objects, and discovered that the foam could be shaped with super-heated wire.

We had some different-sized foam balls made, and because we were convinced we couldn't just sell a small foam ball, we created a broad range of games that employed the balls, such as basketball, dodge ball, indoor baseball, and so on.

Next we headed out to East Longmeadow, Massachusetts, to see Mel Taft and our friends at Milton Bradley, who were doing such a super job with Twister. We were a bit shocked and disappointed when they turned us down. They said they couldn't see adding a toy line to their already extensive line of game and puzzle products.

From there, it was off to Parker Brothers and a visit with their head of new product development,

Henry Simmons. We were disappointed when Henry told us that he had convinced his somewhat reluctant management to test market the basic product—just the ball. And so they did. They called it NERF. To our great surprise, the NERF ball—just a ball in a little square box—sold by the millions. Who knew the world wanted a ball that wouldn't bounce?

The amount of bounce or rebound an object has when it strikes another object is measured by the *coefficient of restitution*, or COR. When we applied for a patent on the NERF ball, one of our major claims was that the ball had a very low COR. It didn't bounce very high, and it was incredibly soft. The promotional copy on the original NERF ball box, released by Parker Brothers in 1969, read "SAFE! The Nerf Ball is made of incredibly soft and spongy synthetic foam. Throw it around indoors; you can't damage lamps or break windows. You can't hurt babies or old people."

SAFE! The **Nerf Ball** is made of incredibly soft and spongy synthetic foam. Throw it around indoors; you can't damage lamps or break windows. You can't hurt babies or old people.

The original NERF ball sold in a box.

Because we had developed a whole line of games and toys that used lightweight foam as the core idea, Parker Brothers didn't want us to take our new foam concepts to other companies. After much consideration, I concluded that Parker Brothers had proven that they were excellent marketers of their products (their most successful game was Monopoly) and, in time, would do a good job of expanding a line of foam products. I agreed to give them the exclusive rights to the idea, and, in return, they agreed that we would participate in all their future foam products. It was definitely a less aggressive move for me and my little company, but it has proven to be a good choice.

People often ask whether NERF was the name that we chose for the wider range of foam products. The answer is no. Our in-house working name while we were developing the product ideas made reference to padding used to enhance women's figures, and so we called it the Falsie Ball. Four or five years after our line of foam products hit the market under the name NERF, we learned where the name came from. One of the people involved in promoting the line suggested naming it after the foam-padded roll bars on Jeeps, which off-roaders had dubbed "NERF bars." The name stuck.

> We took a couple of the foam rocks and started tossing them around. . . . We had inadvertently created the world's first indoor ball!

I still have one of the original foam balls, cut by hand with scissors. During the celebration of the twenty-fifth anniversary of the NERF product line, I used a small mahogany box lined with black velour to display the original ball. It was a useful prop during television interviews. The origin of the NERF line of products came from a common material used to protect fragile objects, found well outside the world of toys.

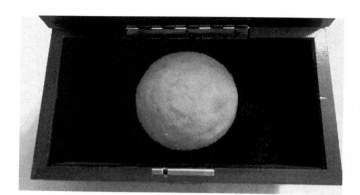

One of the very first polyether foam balls, cut by hand with scissors.

Looking outside is a common practice in toy land. Play-Doh was originally made by a soap company as commercial wallpaper cleaner. The first Slinky toy was a torsion spring designed by a naval engineer to keep sensitive equipment functioning in rough seas. Silly Putty was created as synthetic rubber in a General Electric laboratory. How big are these breakthroughs from outside? Slinky and Silly Putty have each sold over 150 million units around the world, and Hasbro sells 95 million cans of Play-Doh every year.

Looking at other industries shows you that you're not alone.

An additional benefit of looking outside is realizing we're not alone. Many businesspeople spend so much time looking over their shoulder at their competitors that they never take the time to look at their counterparts in other industries. If we know of someone doing exceptional business in our own hometown, maybe we should go find out how they're doing it! As long as we're not a direct competitor, many entrepreneurs enjoy helping like-minded people. The onus is on each of us to move outside. Abraham Lincoln said, "I can learn something from every man I meet." We would do well to go meet them.

* * *

In the late 1970s, I began to be lured by the siren song of yet another industry—a somewhat appropriate pun because it was songwriting that pulled me in this familiar direction. Although I was no stranger to music in the early 1980s, I was decidedly an outsider to the professional music scene when I decided once again to go outside my comfort zone and pursue my dream of writing music. Living in the Twin Cities of Minnesota at the time, I started to hire session players and singers to record some of my original songs. I got to know the regulars at Sound 80, the recording studio in Minneapolis that Prince would eventually make famous.

One day, I played some of the new songs that my friends and I had recorded for my daughter Ree, who always had a keen ear for music. The more songs I played for her, the more she became convinced that some of them deserved a chance to be heard. We both thought one song, "Little Things," written by our good friend Billy Barber, was a hit, but Ree especially had a vision for that song. She befriended another singer-songwriter named Michael Johnson, who had released the hit "Bluer Than Blue" a few years prior. She asked him to lunch and then asked him how to sell songs to record companies. Michael's advice was simple: Go to Nashville.

With twenty songs on a cassette tape, Ree headed to Tennessee to cut her teeth in the tunes trade. She and I ended up making many trips there, working out of hotel rooms for several days at a time. Michael had given us the names of five publishers he knew in Nashville.

"We got in to see every publisher that Michael had suggested to me, but I figured out quickly that they all had their own staff of writers," Ree said. "They didn't care about our songs or our writers as much as I did. So I started to find out who the key producers were in town. My dad and I would get ourselves invited to the parties where we knew industry people would be, and then I'd introduce myself." Ree was twenty-three years old and fearless.

One of our early breaks came when Ree made a big first impression on a Nashville legend named Billy Sherrill. He was the producer who discovered Tammy Wynette and George Jones. He also cowrote "Stand By Your Man," "The Most Beautiful Girl," and many other hit songs.

"I didn't know it at the time, but the man had eighty-five BMI awards," Ree shared. "All I knew was that he was the head of Columbia records, so I went into his office and dropped off a cassette tape of our songs. Literally fifteen minutes later,

I get a call from him. He didn't even say hello. He just barked 'Who the hell are you? Who the hell is Billy Barber? Get your ass back to my office!' He was totally blown away by the songs!"

When she returned to his office, Sherrill told Ree, "You seem like a really nice young woman from the Midwest, so I don't know what the hell you think you're doing in this business. You need to go back to Minneapolis and be a nurse or something."

Of course, Billy was just trying to intimidate her, but Ree was having none of it, and he loved that about her. Later, we heard from Sherrill that our songs sounded different from anything that was being pitched in Nashville at that time. We were outsiders, and that distinction made us stand out in a sea of sameness.

"Up to this point in my life, my dad had been my mentor," Ree said. "He taught me to not be afraid of new challenges. So here I was, in need of guidance, and, without [me] realizing it at the time, Billy Sherrill became my mentor in the music business. I got to learn how to develop my first writer, Billy Barber, alongside a legend. For six months, Billy Sherrill

***

We were outsiders, which made us stand out in a sea of sameness.

helped me learn that art. Ultimately, he couldn't get Billy Barber noticed by pop executives at Columbia Records, so we began pitching his songs to other artists. I will forever be in Billy Sherrill's debt. I think he liked me because I stood up for myself. I remember he wanted 50 percent of the publishing on 'Little Things.' I said, hell no! I worked eighteen months on this song. It's opened every door, and I won't compromise on it." And she never did.

One of the close friends Ree and I made in Nashville was Bob Doyle, who would later go on to manage Garth Brooks. Bob really liked "Little Things." He called Ree one day and told her that The Oak Ridge Boys were looking for songs and their tour bus was idling at their publishing company's office. Ree ran over there and brought them the song.

"I'll never forget that phone call," Ree said. "The day after I crashed onto their bus, they called and promised to release 'Little Things' as the first single off their next record if I would give them 50 percent of the publishing on the song. I refused. I gambled on the belief that they already knew they were going to release it as a single. And guess what? It was the first single off [Step on Out], their next album. It went to number one and spent thirteen weeks on the charts!"

The BMI management team surrounds Reyn, Ree,
and The Oak Ridge Boys.

As outsiders, Ree and I had a number-one single before we had even formed our publishing company. In November of 1985, after "Little Things" became a hit, we officially formed Wrensong and opened our office on Music Row in Nashville.

"Every song we had sounded just different enough to establish us musically," Ree said. "'Little Things' was more of a pop song than a country song. It was outside the norm of Nashville. I ended up getting it cut by The Temptations as well."

Once Wrensong had some success, things changed.

"Initially, the insiders I met in Nashville were like, 'Oh here's this young woman from Minnesota.

She's an outsider who doesn't know anything. Let's help her.' Well, the minute I got my first number one, that all stopped," Ree shared. "I went from confidant to competitor overnight! From then on, we had to stand on our own to prove that our early success wasn't a fluke."

We started with twenty songs, and today we have over three thousand in our catalog. Thirty years later and Wrensong's credits include twelve number-one hit singles, two CMA and ACM Country Music Song of the Year awards, and a Grammy to boot. Then, of course, we have singles from record albums that have sold over sixty million copies for artists such as Reba McEntire, Faith Hill, Kenny Chesney, Carrie Underwood, Ray Charles, Keith Urban, and more.

In 2010, I turned total control of the company over to Ree. Now, as chairman emeritus, I have the great privilege of watching Ree run Wrensong. It's a company we built together, from the outside in.

Idea #5

● ● ● ●

Make It Real: Make One!

"A writer who waits for ideal conditions under which
to work will die without putting a word on paper."

—E. B. White

I've learned that I have to be careful about getting
into social media. I've often found that friends of
friends think I should look at the new game they've
developed or listen to a new song they've written. I'd
like to be helpful, but I've found responding to their
requests really takes time away from my own projects. I'm often approached by entrepreneurs and
wanna-be inventors who want to tell me all about
their next great product or business idea. I always
say the same thing: "Don't tell me. Make one."

When we start making a model of an idea we're
cherishing, that's when the excitement begins.
Waiting to act until we get the idea perfect is often
the biggest mistake we can make. In *Making Ideas*

Happen,[5] Scott Belsky, the founder and CEO of Behance, writes of his time studying IDEO, the renowned design and product innovation company in Palo Alto, California:

> In the process of idea generation in most environments, promising leads become diluted through debate or are simply skipped over during the natural progression of discussion. When a group decides to act upon an idea . . . the team will often strive for consensus before even discussing execution. This search for consensus stalls real progress. . . . [At IDEO,] when team members have an idea for how something might look or function, they'll simply have a prototype built and start tinkering—despite what stage of the design process they are in. IDEO's rapid prototyping practices are part of a clever strategy to overcome some of the biggest boundaries to making ideas happen.

I'm convinced that everyone who breathes has new ideas, but unless those ideas are acted on, they're just notions or nothings. Ideas become something only when they flower into reality.

Why do so many people let their ideas stay

5 Belsky, Scott. *Making Ideas Happen: Overcoming the Obstacles Between Vision & Reality.* New York: Penguin Group, 2010.

My favorite part of the creative process is the moment you think you've got something but you're not quite sure.

stuck right where they bloomed? I think it may be because an idea in our head is pristine, unquestioned, and untested. It's perfect, and it's tempting to avoid the risk of losing it. An idea is much safer locked away in our minds, where it doesn't have to survive the rigorous tests of the real world and either fly or die.

But if it's a toy, we have to play with it. If it's a song, we have to hear it. A story? We have to read it. The only way to prove an idea has possibilities is to make it real and experience it outside our heads. Sure, it takes time and, too often, money and the right connections to see whether an idea is worth pursuing, but there's rarely any reward without risk. As St. Francis of Assisi said, "Start by doing what's necessary, then do what's possible, and, suddenly, you are doing the impossible."

Making an idea real is not only necessary; it's fun! My favorite part of the creative process is the moment when you think you've got something but you're not quite sure. This is when hearts start beating a little faster because we know we have to do something to prove our idea right or wrong, useful or useless. Can the idea hold water even when you're trying to poke holes in it? Can it survive examination from your friends? Coworkers? Family? Trusted advisors? In order to test the idea, we have to make a working model or prototype.

I still have fond memories of my staff and me sitting at our drafting tables in the Winsor Concept offices, snipping away at chunks of polyester foam blocks to make different-size foam balls. This was, of course, right after we had realized the potential in using foam materials to make the fun that became NERF. As a group, we had decided to make the idea real. Our rough round balls looked like ragged rocks, but they served their purpose. We quickly became convinced that they had fun properties no other ball had. We bounced them on the ground, over nets, and off each other's heads!

No one in the toy and game business would think of taking a product to retail without extensive play testing. Watching people play with a new idea not only tells us whether people like it or not, but also often allows the weak points in the idea to be identified and corrected. And without a working model that really functions, play testing is impossible. If I hadn't immediately made a prototype of my "the players are the game pieces" idea and gathered colleagues and friends to play it, the concept might have stayed in my head and never progressed. As it turned out, that first impetuous test was solid proof that the concept was worth chasing, and eventually, Twister was born.

Happy Accidents

Another benefit of making a prototype is that ideas often take on a life of their own. We often think we're developing an idea in a certain direction, when, suddenly, it leads us to a totally different—and often more interesting—idea than our original concept. Certainly, NERF and Twister are prime examples of this phenomenon.

When I was about ten years old, my friends and I would often spend rainy summer afternoons playing Monopoly. Before I ever dreamed that I would spend my adult years devising new toy and game ideas, I decided that the Monopoly game board needed an extra path. I wanted to make it possible

A prototype will often take on a life of its own.

for a player who was down and almost out, to get back in the game or lose it all. So, between the spaces for the Reading and Short Line railroads, I drew another path and called it "Chancey Lane." I made nine landing spaces. If a player landed on the middle space, they would win two thousand dollars. Two other spaces sent the player to the Go space. But landing on any of the other six spaces meant the player lost all their money and/or all their properties—all or nothing. I had no idea whether "Chancey Lane" was an option that my friends—or even I—would ever use. But, sure enough, it didn't take long before our whole gang wouldn't play a game of Monopoly without it. And it all began when I took out a pen and drew an extra path on an existing game board.

In the spring of 2013, when my knees had reached a pain threshold that led me to use my sand-wedge golf club as a cane, I consulted with my good friend Dr. Jack McMahon. Jack is a retired, renowned orthopedist who quickly guided me to a young colleague of his, Dr. Mark Heller, whom he had taught a unique technique for replacing worn out hips and knees with new titanium ones. The next thing I knew, I was lying in a hospital bed with two new knees and wondering what the hell I had gotten myself into. But I was a good boy and did my rehab exercises, and now, as long as you don't ask me to play striker on your soccer team, I can move pretty much pain free.

Titanium knees. I knew that the doctors had pounded the metal rods into my shin- and thigh-bones. What I didn't know until recently was that the titanium rod in each of my legs is now fused with my bones. Unbelievable! Whoever figured that one out?

In 1952 a Swedish researcher named Per-Ingvar Branemark stumbled onto the concept.[6] I say *stumbled* because he was trying to study how blood flows through bone structures by inserting a titanium tube into a rabbit's leg. When the experiment was over, he tried to remove the tube, only to find that it and the bone had fused. No other metal or plastic material had ever done that. Branemark apparently understood immediately what had happened, and, to his great credit, he chose to do something about his discovery. He spent the rest of his life experimenting with various ways that titanium and human bone could bond. He called it *osseointegration*. Today, titanium is used for dental implants, new hips, and new knees, and it provides an aging population with a miraculous new lease on life.

* * *

---

6 Lewin, Tamar. "Per-Ingvar Branemark, Dental Innovator, Dies at 85." *New York Times*, December 27, 2014.

I have a friend of a Southern persuasion who likens the pursuit of any creative endeavor to "riding the wild pony." Maybe that's an over-the-top analogy, but his point is a valid one. When you're excited to have locked onto a new idea, you may think you know where it's going, but it can fool you and suddenly head off in a new direction. If you panic, you'll get thrown, and your idea will be lost. But if you're willing to follow the twists and turns your idea may take, you may just be in for the ride of your life.

In 1829, a preacher by the name of Reverend Sylvester Graham ministered to a devoted batch of parishioners who were apparently attentive to his every idea. And one of his ideas was that the sexual appetites of his flock could—and should—be suppressed through a diet of bland foods. Being a man with some entrepreneurial ambition, he baked a batch of rather mild crackers. In all modesty, he

---

When you lock onto a new idea, you may think you know where it's going, but it can fool you and suddenly head off in a new direction.

dubbed them *graham crackers*.[7] To his delight, his dutiful congregation thought quite highly of his creation, and, lo and behold, so did some people who

Ideas have to be put to work. To do that, we have to make one.

discovered the Reverend's cracker boxes on retail shelves. Devouring graham crackers to curb carnal appetites may not have worked as the Reverend intended, but because he rode the wild pony, today we can all enjoy a s'more by the campfire. That's one happy accident!

The moment we decide to pursue ideas may be impetuous, inspired, or intentional. But whatever your approach, those ideas have to be put to work. And to do that, we must first make them real. We have to make one.

7   Vodrey, Catherine S. "Sweet Cracker Legacy of Sylvester Graham's Crusade for Healthful Living." *Pittsburgh Post-Gazette*, August 9, 2001.

Idea #6

● ● ● ●

Be Open

"The mind is like a parachute. It functions only when open."
—Author Unknown

Nearly every successful product, company, or creative endeavor my teams have produced ended up in
a place very different from where we were initially
headed. We set out to create a game, and we ended
up with NERF, the world's first indoor ball. I set out
to create a promotion for shoe polish, and we ended
up with Twister. I've had people suggest that it must
take patience and fearlessness to allow yourself,
your team, or your company to deviate from an ini-
tial goal. I'd like to claim those attributes, but, in
my experience, it's more like the old joke, "When
you get to a fork in the road, take it." Usually when
a project has run out of options, it comes to a dead
end. At that time, the common choice is to abandon
ship. Yet when this apparent dead end has greeted
our teams, we've been open to looking for unusual

applications for the core idea. Being open has often turned our dead ends into detours and set us off in a direction that ended up being well worth the trip.

I allow new directions to overtake me all the time when writing songs, because so many happy accidents occur when I am willing to leave myself open to unusual opportunities. In my experience, a good song usually has several good lines and maybe even several good hooks in it, any one of which could end up being a new song better than the original. I've not had much success forcing a song or product in a preconceived direction. Instead, I consider the method of ideation a much more organic process—it's a river more than a paved road. Sure, there are times when an idea seems to know exactly where it's going and when that direction is dead ahead, but that's rare. More times than not, our best ideas have developed along circuitous routes.

One day I stumbled onto the phrase "people have never been more like they are now." I knew I had to use it in a humorous song. By the time I had

Ideation is an organic process. It's a river more than a paved road.

pulled two verses together, I had developed a story song about the strangest man I've ever met. He sat outside the gate to a mission church and begged people to put coins onto his small green plate. Prominent people from all over the world came to hear his words of wisdom, captured in the chorus of the song:

Well, people never been more like they are now
Since I can't remember when.
I ain't never seen life more like this
No matter where I've been.
And life's gonna get more like it'll be
So you know just what's in store.
Things are more like they are today
Than they've ever been before
Things are more like they are today
Than they've ever been before

It's such a treat to be surprised by the process of where ideas begin and where they end. Being open to the surprises that unfold is where we find what I call "The Rush."

As I've already mentioned, when I assembled the team for Winsor Concepts, I wanted to encourage openness and interaction. So I arranged our drawing tables and workstations to face each other in a large circle. Maybe it was naive to presume we could replicate the success of Twister, and I had some misgivings. With five kids in good schools, I recall the pressure of not knowing whether the money I needed to run the company would be there each month. But at the same time, I woke up happy each day, knowing I'd be trying to invent a new toy or game and not an in-store display. We worked hard, and, less than two years after the success of Twister, we created and licensed the NERF ball to Parker Brothers. Without being open to that risk, and without my father being open to change (letting me separate myself from the core display business), that success wouldn't have been possible.

Be Open to Movement

In 1988, Nike launched one of the most successful advertising campaigns in history. "Just Do It" was so effective, marketing gurus say, because it was a call to action that was at once universal and intensely personal. I liked it because what it said to me was "Move!" We all know many creative people who wait for inspiration to strike before they move into action. As I look back, I realize that some of my luckiest moments have happened when I've chosen to move first.

There's a great scene in *Butch Cassidy and the Sundance Kid* in which Sundance, played by Robert Redford, is asked to prove he's a good shot. On his first attempt, he fires from a standing position and misses the target.

●◦●◦●

Some of my luckiest moments have happened when I've chosen to move first.

Then he asks, "Can I move?"

His evaluator starts to question his question when Sundance suddenly drops, draws, and fires all in one motion, obliterating his target with successive shots.

"I'm better when I move," he explains simply. I think we all are.

I'm convinced that the ideas that I've been blessed with are gifts. And when I come upon them—or they come upon me—I have an obligation to try to bring them into to the world. No doubt this sounds childishly naive to some, and maybe it is. All I know is that I often ask for guidance to use the gifts I'm given wisely and well.

My kids and coworkers cower in fear when I say, "Hey, I've got this idea . . . "

Their response is usually something like, "Yeah, sure, here he goes again!" But I'm not getting any younger, and I still have a bunch of ideas I want to get out into the world. So I simply start. Like Sundance, I'm better when I move.

Be Open to Serendipity

I'm not sure I'll ever know whether inspiration is a result of plain-old blind luck or whether ideas arrive as part of one of those gifts I mentioned above. Either way, I'm happy to tap into the wellspring.

I'm not a big fan of having my cell phone run my life. I treat it as a convenience, not a constant. If I'm connected to my phone at all times, I'm disconnected from the world right in front of me, where serendipity is at play. A chance meeting in the hotel elevator during a conference may be more beneficial to me than any presentation from the stage. A clever comment or funny interaction I overhear on vacation may spark my next song or game idea.

One afternoon, in a bar outside of Stanford, Montana, Mary and I had gathered with some friends for lunch. I sidled up to the bar to get some beers for the group, and next to me were two local ranchers. I couldn't help but hear them sharing their plans for the forthcoming winter.

"You stickin' around all winter?" asked one of them.

"Nope," replied his friend. "I'm takin' off, and let the bugs all eat the barley."

I couldn't wait to get back to the table to write that conversation on a napkin. I'm happy to say that "bugs and barley" inspired the chorus of a song on one of the Curly Lasagna albums Jeff Harrington and I wrote.

> *I took off and let the bugs all eat my barley.*
> *I left and let the hoppers eat my corn.*
> *I ate my pride and hitched a ride to Kansas City,*
> *Feelin' sorry for myself and so forlorn.*

I know a stand-up comic who relies on serendipity as his method of mining for material. He regularly schedules time to walk around his city, open to whatever he may see or hear that could trigger an idea for a joke. He contends that new jokes, like songs, live in the interactions happening all around us. The added benefit of his method is that he feels fully alive and connected to the world around him when he's living his practice.

Put the Pot on Simmer

I'd be derelict if I didn't mention another technique I love to use. There are times when I'm trying to think through a problem, and something seems to be blocking the idea's progress. It's like the idea is in a pot with a lot of other information, and the harder I stir and the hotter the pot gets, the further I get from a solution. What to do? I put the pot on simmer and leave the kitchen. I go do something else.

I know a couple of very good songwriters who hop into a car and drive around town whenever their writing sessions hit a roadblock. That's the way they leave the kitchen, and they swear by the results.

So go fishing, running, golfing, swimming or, yes, take a nap. That's what I'm told Thomas Edison did. He had a dilapidated old cot next to the desk in his office. When the answer wasn't coming to him, he'd hit the cot for twenty minutes. And he claims that he was astounded by the number of times the answer was there when he awoke. I'm no Edison, but I often get great results from putting the project on simmer and leaving the kitchen.

Be Open to Learning

In order to accomplish the seemingly simple suggestion of being open to learning, we have to first admit that we don't have all the answers. In his excellent book, *Creativity, Inc.*,[8] Ed Catmull, the cofounder of Pixar Animation Studios, writes,

---

8   Catmull, Ed, with Amy Wallace. *Creativity, Inc.: Overcoming the Unseen Forces That Stand in the Way of True Inspiration.* New York: Random House, 2014.

I believe the best managers acknowledge and make room for what they do not know—not just because humility is a virtue, but because until one adopts that mindset, the most striking breakthroughs cannot occur. . . . Moreover, successful leaders embrace the reality that their models may be wrong or incomplete. Only when we admit what we don't know can we ever hope to learn it.

Catmull gets it right. I don't really think of myself as humble, but I suspect my dyslexia has helped me be convinced I'm not the smartest person in any meeting. So I've gotten used to encouraging everyone I'm working with to pitch in. The same sense of not being sure that I'm right has led me to be curious.

On a day-to-day basis, I'm drawn to magazine articles that tell me something I didn't know before. My magazine racks are stacked with an eclectic mix, from *The Week* and *Golf Digest* to *National Geographic* and *Rolling Stone*. We all struggle to stay up with current trends, and magazines are helpful for that purpose. They encourage and satisfy my curiosity and, at the same time, keep me energized.

Be Open to a Calling

I taught myself to draw by watching the artists I worked with at my father's company. I took pads of tracing paper home at night to practice. I'd place the tracing paper over an ad in a magazine and sketch in the shaded parts I could see through the paper until a picture emerged. When I lifted the tracing paper away—voilà—there was a pretty darned good sketch of the ad. Soon I could draw whatever I wanted by focusing on the shadows and dark shapes first. Before I knew it, the forms that I observed were captured on paper. Over the next fifteen years, I kept honing my drawing skills and actually improved to the point that I had a couple of shows of my watercolors in small galleries.

In 1973, the product line of the NERF toys had grown and provided the Winsor Concepts team a reputation as a respected toy and game development group. But since the introduction of the NERF line in 1969, we had not succeeded in placing any other ideas with toy or game companies. With a

⬤ ◦ ⬤ ⬤

If something didn't pan out,
I could try something else.
And so I did.

growing sense of frustration, I concluded that this particular mix of personalities had achieved great success, but maybe it was time to back off. I was very fond of all of my teammates at this point, so I decided to give each of them a percentage of the NERF royalties for three years. Most of them had families to feed, and the royalties provided a more than adequate fund that allowed them to take their time to find new jobs that they really loved.

Be Open to Change

I'm aware that my decision to close down the Winsor Concepts company appeared—and still appears—to be a very abrupt change of occupations. As I reflect on my decision, I'm pretty sure that my ability to pull away from the family business and start Winsor Concepts gave me the freedom to make the same kind of choice again. I didn't have to run a point-of-purchase advertising company all my life, and neither did I have to focus my career on being a toy and game inventor or designer. Being open to change meant I could also be an artist, and if that didn't pan out, I could try something else. And so I did.

I closed the Winsor Concepts office and decided to strike out in a new direction. If I was ever going to have a time to answer the call of becoming a visual artist, this was my best opportunity. My capabilities as an artist had been improving, and I began to envision two themes I hoped to explore. So, once again, I opened the door to something new.

I found a 3,600-square-foot space with perfect northern light in a building filled with a mix of professional and amateur graphic artists. The Rossmor Building in St. Paul was my creative home for the next eight years. I painted in my studio for at least eight hours a day, five days a week, and the two themes that had drawn me to this place began to emerge. The first theme grew out of a fascination with water and its variety of moods and appearances. The second I chose to call Continuums.

My first Continuums were seven-foot-long watercolors. Over time, I went on to develop a process of applying acrylic paint to primed and untreated Masonite that involved laying down and blending colors in a prismatic progression. I also developed a unique method of laying down and later removing rubber cement as a masking technique to add spatial depth to the paintings. The Caterpillar Corporation in Peoria, Illinois, commissioned me to create a ten-foot-long painting and, later, a fourteen-foot Continuum wall sculpture made of Masonite that appeared to be woven ribbons of colors that progressed prismatically. I attached a small framed footnote beside the ten-foot-long piece when it was hung on the wall of the computer center. The note invited individuals and team members to stand before the painting and point out where they felt their current project was on the Continuum. Hopefully it sparked some dialogue around the project.

A worker puts the final touches on the installation of the fourteen-foot-long Continuum.

One of several ten-foot-long Continuums.

My explorations convinced me that the large-scale universe we saw through the world's most powerful telescopes were very similar to the small-scale universe we saw through the lenses of our most powerful microscopes. My Continuum paintings were all accomplished between 1973 and 1979. When the color-filtered images of the Hubble telescope started to be unveiled to us all in 1990 and the following decades, I was delighted to find that my Continuum images were amazingly similar.

I would occasionally make appointments with some of the significant private art galleries in New York City. I'd walk in with slides of my work, and as I passed the very intellectual art on the walls, something told me that my stuff wasn't what they were looking for. That turned out to be right, and after eight years of intense focus on the two themes that I felt called to create, it was clear to me that in the existing art climate, my work was not finding an audience. Yet I was satisfied that I had indeed created enough work to say what I wanted to say. I look back on that time with great fondness. I feel I grew as an artist and a person, and I'm very glad I was open to answering that call.

I have a wildly artistic friend who recently had an epiphany that shook her to the core. After thirty years of being a very successful computer artist and graphic designer, she was arranging her studio and came across some of her old paintings. As she looked through them, she smiled and thought, "Wow, I was good." Then a palpable wave of regret washed over her, and she slumped to the floor and wept. She had spent too many years making art solely to feed her family, instead of also making art to feed her soul. It had been such a slow and subtle change that she hadn't noticed it. She decided to make a change. I am happy to report that her studio is now dominated by canvases instead of computers, and she finds that she's even more productive at work now that she's open to getting lost in play.

Idea #7

● ● ● ●

Finding The Rush

"The secret of genius is to carry the spirit of the child into old age, which means never losing your enthusiasm."
—Aldous Huxley

For over fifty years, I have had the great privilege of spending my days playing for a living. I don't mean that I goof off. I work pretty hard at play every day. Some would call that enthusiasm. I call it The Rush, and I've been chasing that feeling all my life. Am I addicted to this feeling? Perhaps, but so far my family and friends haven't attempted an intervention. I simply love to be a part of bringing new ideas to the world, and when I feel The Rush, I'm pretty sure I'm on to something new and exciting.

I'm fascinated by the work of Dr. Teresa M. Amabile, a professor of business administration and the director of research at Harvard Business

School.[9] Her research focuses on what drives creativity and, just as important, what kills it. She has found that extrinsic motivation—or motivation that comes from outside a person, such as money, the lure of job advancement, and so on—does not foster creativity as well as intrinsic motivation does. Amabile has found that when people are intrinsically motivated to engage in their work for the sheer challenge and enjoyment of it, they are more likely to come up with better creative solutions.

I've been chasing The Rush all my life.

It's interesting that the old carrot-and-stick management method is still employed so often by managers of salespeople: "Sell more cars, and you'll win a trip to the Bahamas." "Fail to meet your quota, and you're fired!" But I'll bet that the car salesperson who is constantly dreaming up ways to attract new customers is the one who wakes up in the morning most excited to get to the office.

9 Amabile, Teresa M., and Steve J. Kramer. "1: What Really Motivates Workers" in "The HBR List: Breakthrough Ideas for 2010." *Harvard Business Review* 88, no. 1/2 (January–February 2010): 44–45.

For me, the challenge and excitement of trying to bring new ideas into the world still has me excited to get to my work studio. It's pretty simple: That's a place where I can find The Rush.

* * *

When I was in my twenties and recently married, I was a scratch golfer. I enjoyed playing amateur golf and, in a five-year span, won my country club championship three times. But I found that new babies at home and a busy travel schedule were getting in the way of my golf game. It didn't take me long to get it straight.

With some help from my wife, Mary, I concluded that the country club had to go. My golfing buddies thought I was crazy. I was certain that I would miss golf, but I quickly found out that I really didn't. Oh, I missed the camaraderie, but I didn't miss the intensity of maintaining a low handicap. In addition, I discovered the more precious resource called time. I now had more of it to devote to my family and my creative activities. I have never regretted the decision to put my golf game on the shelf.

When I was in my mid-fifties, I found I had some time to retry my hand at the game. I joined a national senior golf organization and even won four club championships over the next two decades. Today most of my friends are retired, and they play golf three or four times a week. I try to find time join them once or occasionally twice a week, and I love the laughs we enjoy.

It's interesting to me to realize that when I was playing the game competitively, the lure of the game was actually a form of The Rush. There's a wonderful excitement that takes hold of me and all golfers when we play tournaments where every shot counts and, near the end, we're in the hunt. After three major knee operations, that kind of golf intensity isn't available to me anymore. But I consider myself fortunate to be able to enjoy The Rush of working on new ideas.

*   *   *

Over the years, I've discovered that I'm a visual learner. Looking back on the many activities I've been involved with, I've come to realize that, somehow, I've always had the ability to see solutions or connections that others might not have. Perhaps it's the way my dyslexic brain is wired, or maybe I developed this ability as a way to cope with my dyslexia. I really don't know. Either way, I now see this ability (or coping mechanism) as a great advantage. It helps me stay very enthusiastic about my work. Quite often, I can see where I'm headed, and I can't wait to get there. I tend to get bogged down if I try to think in a methodical, linear "A, B, C, D" fashion.

Somehow I've developed the ability to see to the end and to turn my ABCs into AB . . . Zs.

* * *

Somehow, I've always had the ability to see solutions that others might not have.

In *The Dyslexic Advantage*,[10] Drs. Brock and Fernette Eide write that "the percentage of dyslexic professionals in fields such as engineering, art, and entrepreneurship is over twice the percentage of dyslexic individuals in the general population." One of the major conclusions of their research is that dyslexia need not be looked on as a disability. In fact, people with dyslexia have certain intrinsic abilities that give them a skill set the general population doesn't enjoy.

* * *

Sometimes, I feel The Rush when I'm just having fun. I was playing backyard croquet with some

---

10 Eide, Brock L., and Fernette F. Eide. *The Dyslexic Advantage: Unlocking the Hidden Potential of the Dyslexic Brain.* New York: Plume, 2011.

friends one day, and I realized the game has a very big flaw: It's boring when it's not your turn. The game had not changed with the times, and its pace was painfully slow. So I decided that there must be a better way to enjoy an afternoon with friends using mallets and balls.

●●●●

Sometimes, I feel The Rush when I'm just having fun.

After fifty-plus years as a developer of games, I've concluded that the most fun games are the ones that allow every player to be involved in every other player's turn. Backyard croquet does not have that attribute. So I turned to my magic words: *What happens if* each team has some pegs that they have to protect while simultaneously trying to knock over the opposing team's pegs? We kept asking these types of questions and refined the rules to create an outdoor lawn game we call King's Court.

It's a real treat for me to watch teams playing King's Court having fun while strategizing and debating their next move. Should we defend? Should we attack? It all seems so simple once the game begins to work. But, as we all know, the biggest successes occur when an idea is boiled down to its simplest form. In King's Court, every player is involved in every other player's turn.

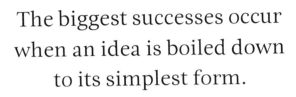

The biggest successes occur when an idea is boiled down to its simplest form.

In Idea #2: *What Happens if . . .* , I described how Jeff Harrington and I built a catalog of stories and songs for kids called Curly Lasagna that we hoped would also be enjoyed by parents. Talk about The Rush! It's hard for me to quantify the amount of fun it was to record and rerecord these stories and songs. Bringing all the material to life by singing all the voices in our recording studio? What a privilege! Believe me, I often wonder how I became the guy who gets to play while he's supposed to be working.

Start with the Ending

One of the benefits of writing this book is that it has afforded me the fun of sharing the methods and techniques I've used in my working career. I can see more clearly the approaches I've taken to problem solving—that is to say, the way I think. As I pointed out earlier, I now am even more aware that what I habitually do is visualize the end result of an idea. When I ask myself that marvelous question—*what happens if*—it often takes me into the future, where I can foresee the outcome. Once I'm back in the present, the next words out of my mouth are usually, "Okay, how do we get there?" As a result, I don't set goals in the traditional sense. Writing out lists in a linear, methodical fashion doesn't work for me. I'm much more effective when I can apply my ability to visualize the solution or end result of an idea and then take action to get there.

When I was in school, I had a very hard time taking notes during a lecture. Somehow, my mind didn't allow me to discern what was important and what wasn't. I'd look around at all the other students and wonder, *What on earth are they all writing down?* I was just waiting for the professor to make a point. It seemed like I wrote down the big picture, and my fellow classmates wrote down every word! I may have gotten the main point of the lecture, but I missed a lot of the details that the professor would quiz us on later.

Albert Einstein once said, "Everybody is a genius. But if you judge a fish by its ability to climb a tree, it will live its whole life believing that it is stupid." I wasn't a very good student, but I knew I wasn't stupid.

My high school Latin teacher, Al Smith, was one of a kind. He wore light blue shirts with a popular comic book character (Andy Gump) on the front pocket. He wouldn't wash his car until the day before he sold it, and his gathering call to study hall was, "Come get a head-u-cate!" The only way he could describe the quandary I posed for him as a student was to tell me that I had "low cunning."

Like every human being who has ever graced this planet, I wish I'd known then what I know now. But I've found some consolation in learning that to keep my rush from turning into a rut, I need to focus on what I do best and what really turns me on.

———— ●●●● ————

I wish I'd known then what I know now—to focus on my strengths instead of dwelling on my weaknesses.

Over the years, I've found that salesmanship is not my strength, nor is selling how I wish to spend my time. I love ideas, but I don't want to sell them. I'm pretty sure it's because I have a very hard time listening to someone pick apart the ideas I've worked (and played) so hard to develop. Chuck Foley was a big help when we presented what became the game Twister to Milton Bradley. Norton Cross was my sales manger at Winsor Concepts and helped me sell NERF to Parker Brothers. Charlie Girsch was my salesman for Team Winsor, and now my daughter Katie sells my toy and game ideas for Reyn Guyer Design. Tom Guyer is the lead voice for the Winsor Learning company, and the songwriters at Wrensong Music rely on Ree Buchanan to get their songs on the albums that country music stars are making. By focusing on what I love to do and what I do best, my work is much more fun.

The Rush has a strange dichotomy to it. It's work but also play, struggle but also fun. It's a challenge, but it's also an accomplishment. It closely resembles a state of optimal experience called *flow*, in which a person performing a challenging activity is fully immersed, energized, and focused. Psychologist Mihaly Csikszentmihalyi coined the phrase. In *Flow: The Psychology of Optimal Experience*,[11] he writes,

> The best moments in our lives are not the passive, receptive, relaxing times—although such experiences can also be enjoyable, if we have worked hard to attain them. The best moments usually occur when a person's body

---

11 Csikszentmihalyi, Mihaly. *Flow: The Psychology of Optimal Experience*. New York: Harper and Row, 1990.

or mind is stretched to its limits in a voluntary effort to accomplish something difficult and worthwhile.

Flow is more vocation than vacation. Don't get me wrong; I enjoy shutting my work down and relaxing my mind, and I make sure that I do it regularly. But the idea of retirement is ludicrous, because I love what I do, and there's nothing I'd rather do than feel The Rush of working with new ideas. It's a source of great joy in my life.

Please allow me to turn a concept attributed to an unknown author into a verse:

> *I love to lose myself*
> *in what I do,*
> *and I often find*
> *myself there, too.*

If you've read this book to the end, then I'm sure that you, too, have experienced the feeling of excitement when you suddenly come upon a new idea. For all of us, it's there for the taking. Let's enjoy The Rush.

About the Authors

Reyn Guyer

Reyn Guyer is a native of St. Paul, Minnesota. He and his wife, Mary, have five children, ten grandchildren, and two great-grandchildren. Reyn is a serial entrepreneur in a variety of creative fields, including toys and games, music publishing, education, and art.

Reyn's career began in 1967, when he and his team developed and licensed the game Twister to Milton Bradley. In 1969, he developed the NERF ball and licensed it and its many offshoots to Parker Brothers. In 1986, Reyn was inducted into the Hasbro Inventor's Hall of Fame.

Reyn's love for music led him to cofound Wrensong Music in 1985. The publishing company has had many number-one singles and won a Grammy and two CMA Song of the Year awards.

Having struggled with dyslexia himself, Reyn cofounded Winsor Learning in 1991 to help children who also struggle to read. The Sonday System and Let's Play Learn are effective remediation methods for students who are behind in their reading skills. These programs are used in hundreds of school systems across the country.

Other projects that keep Reyn busy include:

- The Curly Lasagna project, a series of stories and songs for kids and parents that he created with Jeff Harrington
- The musical *Stained Glass*, also cowritten with Jeff Harrington
- The new dice game Rally Roll, which he invented in 2014
- Creating sculptures and artwork, many of which are in private collections
- Doing croquet one better with a new lawn game called King's Court

Tim Walsh

Tim Walsh lives in Sarasota, Florida, with his wife and two daughters. He designed or codesigned games that have sold over seven million copies in twenty-five countries. Tim first wrote of Reyn's success with toys in *Timeless Toys*,[12] which was praised by *The Wall Street Journal* and *USA Today*. Tim's second ode to toys, *WHAM-O Super-Book* (Chronicle Books, 2008), was selected by National Public Radio as "one of the best gift books of the year."

Tim served as creative consultant and editor for the documentary film *Toyland*, in which Reyn appears. The film won "best documentary" in three US film festivals. He is the coproducer of *Buzz Heard 'Round the World: The Inventor of Operation and the Power of Play*, a documentary film that will debut in 2016.

As a speaker and presenter, Tim believes that play has the power to engage and connect all of us, and that play is the lifeblood of organizations that want to collaborate and create more. He considers his collaboration with Reyn on this book to be a career highlight and credits much of his own success in toys and publishing to Reyn's mentorship. The two have known each other for twelve years.

---

12 Walsh, Tim. *Timeless Toys: Classic Toys and the Playmakers Who Created Them*. Kansas City: Andrews-McMeel, 2005.

52615405R00084

Made in the USA
Charleston, SC
18 February 2016